Printed in the United States of America

First Printing, 2012

ISBN 978-1-105-51302-2

Men Just Don't Get It!

The Alice & Lucille

Tell It Like It Is

Play Book for Men

Welcome to the Pick-Up Game!

If you have picked up this book you are curious. Curious about what two women could possibly have as advice for men. This is not a book about relationships, dating or even getting to know someone of the opposite sex. Consider this book an instruction manual on how to get that woman you meet tonight to go home with you. Or to have her take YOU home. The point is, sometimes things are going great and you turn around, she's blowing you off and you don't know what happened. Where did she go? This should help you along the road of the successful pick-up. Take our word for it… we will show you how to have her saying, "Yes, please!" instead of, "Hell, No!"

Chapter 1: Hell No!

These are the simple observations of two single women and where men make their biggest mistakes in the game of the pickup. While all events are completely factual (yes, we swear!), names have been omitted to protect the (not so) innocent and some events have had the language toned down quite a bit – you know, just in case our mothers ever read this. If you recognize yourself in this commentary, the odds are pretty good that this was written especially for you & perhaps even about you. Maybe you will learn something to help you with your game, or maybe you will just have a really good laugh. Believe me, we did!

***

"Chances"

He spies a woman at the end of the bar. She is beautiful & he finds himself very attracted to her. She is engrossed in conversation with everyone around her. She is the life of the party. He edges over and joins in the conversation. She freely includes him. He is mesmerized. He seeks her out again later that evening, she is dancing. She dances with him. He opens his mouth and says, "So , do I have any chance at all?"

Game Over. Men just do not get it.

What men have failed to understand since the beginning of time is that a woman wants to be pursued. What is more fun than a good chase? Take, for instance, your household cat. They chase a mouse around the house. Pounce! Capturing it lightly and ever so gently with their paws and mouth, then playing with it only to let it go to chase again. A woman wants to feel desired. If she has to make the decision (which was already made the moment she spied you across the bar) vocally, you will never succeed - whether it is just for the night or for a pursued relationship.

"Open Mouth, Insert Foot"

He sees her; a tall blonde, slender build with long legs. He's really attracted to long legs on a lady! He thinks she is so cute as she is laughing & swaying to the music. His brother is talking to her friend, a delightful brunette, and he is diggin' on the blonde. He thinks to himself, "It doesn't get much better than this … Picture, we need a picture! The guys back home will never believe she's my vacation hook up!" Then he shouts aloud, "I need a picture with the *big* girl!"

Game Over. Men just do not get it.

Ok really?!?! If this even needs an explanation men are even denser than women had even considered. All women want to feel small next to the man of their choice. They want to feel like at any moment you could completely ravage them and they could not stop you. They want to look up into your eyes as you grab them tightly and take total control. Calling her the big girl? Sorry buddy, you may as well fold your hand now.

<u>“Sneezy”</u>

He eyes a cute gal at the piano bar and graciously asks to sit down next to her. By some miracle she says yes. He begins to inch closer on his stool hoping to overhear some conversation he might be able to include himself in. But what is that? A sneeze coming! Quickly he pulls out his handkerchief and “ACHOO!” too late to turn his head away, leaves a spray of your spittle down her back. A complete look of disgust appears on her face. So what did he do then? He thinks to himself, “Maybe if I sit here long enough she will just forget it happened.”

Men REALLY don’t get it.

Good manners always go a long way. Didn’t your mom ever tell you this? Word of advice, if you are sniffling, sneezing, coughing, and aching (sound like a familiar commercial?) don’t go out thinking you are going to score. I don’t want what you have, whatever that might be. There is nothing attractive about flu-like symptoms. It does not make some mothering instinct come out in me or make me want to take care of you. Go to bed and live to fight another day.

“Playground”

She is at the pool. Lounging in a bikini with her friends, she is soaking in the sun. The young man passing by really would like to get her attention, but how?! Smoothly, he approaches and using both of his index fingers points them at her & says “pow”… then hanging his head and mumbling “I can’t believe I just did that.” He scurries away.

Men just don’t get it.

While this may be cute on some level, there are two critical mistakes being made. First, playing ‘bang bang’ should be reserved for those 10 and under (or perhaps even in the bedroom if you can get her that far). Second, hanging your head & mumbling is always a no-no… even when you screw up, confidence is your best way out.

“Gawkers”

He enters a fancy restaurant with two beautiful women. Maybe they are his sister and his cousin. On the other hand, maybe one of them is his wife. He glances up to see across the room a table for two and notices that being seated in his direct line of view are two attractive women. He stares openly. Never once removing his gaze even when his tablemates, whoever they may be, try to speak to him. They notice the fixation. Both the women he is seated with & the women he is staring at notice. Does he ever stop staring or look away? Absolutely not.

Men just do not get it.

A glance and a little smile off and on across a crowded room are acceptable & flirtatiously fun if it's reciprocated! Staring and gawking constantly throughout a 2 hour meal is not. Bottom line, she now believes you are most likely a stalker or perhaps a serial killer.

“The Friends”

He’s an entertainer. He loves the spotlight & the stage, but more than that – he really loves the ladies & hopes that one day it might just pay off in the biggest way. Finally, the night of his dreams arrives & there are no longer simply couples waiting on him to tickle those ivories. Ahhh, the good-looking girls have arrived, but wait – he sees they have a chaperone along. They are with a man friend, but only one between them? Thinking to himself, “This can't be, because I want both!” He begins to pout. ... What should he do? He pauses to consider his options. Then - Yes! He has found a solution! Determined now, he proclaims he will enchant them with his song! (Of course when they are not looking he will roll his eyes at their friend!) He believes the male friend will be so intimidated by his presence at the piano & ability to work the crowd that he will disappear and they will stay. Naturally, the ladies will praise his prowess then throw themselves at his feet!

Men just don't get it.

Gentlemen, we are here to tell you that your way ‘in’ with women will be to acknowledge & even become friendly with the man they have chosen to spend time with. Even if your plan is to later weasel yourself into that same picture, you must realize that if they have entered the venue with him voluntarily, they will consider him an ally. Use this to your advantage, do not alienate him. If he starts feeling uncomfortable like you are moving in on his territory, she may just drop him like a hot potato. No woman ever wants to feel smothered.

<u>"The Waiting Game"</u>

He walks into the bar and can feel eyes upon him. This exceptional woman is slowly eyeing him up and down. She smiles seductively. He makes eye contact. The fire between the two of them is literally smoldering. What is his first move? Walk out the door to come back. When he returns, she is gone. Where did she go?!?! How come she did not sit around waiting for him? Didn't she feel the same? Maybe he imagined it.

Men just don't get it.

Take a cue from that famous 1960's English rock band on this one, boys… they had it right all along. C'mon, you know the song! Something about wanting it & going to get it! Sing along with me now… la la lala la la la lalalala.

You are hot and you know it. You KNOW I noticed. Don't walk away. If I have looked at you like you are the only bottle of water in the Sahara desert and you have returned the gaze in a similar manner, your best approach is to head to the bar and order a drink. Let me get a closer look at you. I might just start a conversation, and you just might get lucky. If you walk away I will find something else to do. I am not saying you should be engrossed with me and ruin all these fun flirty glances by making a mad dash to my side and never leaving. Hang around, make eye contact, and give me slow private smiles from across the bar for awhile. Trust me; I will be putty in your hands. Don't waste my time, and I guarantee I will not waste yours.

“Cheap Whine”

He and his wingman are at their usual hangout, a hotel bar in a tourist zone (in their own town of course). It's always been their hot spot for picking up on the ladies. It’s been a long night & it’s getting late when suddenly, two nice looking women enter the bar & have a seat a few chairs away. He makes eye contact and comes over to say hello. The chatter is light and fun. He thinks, hey – this might not be such a bad night after all! The conversation turns to wine and one of the women mention her interest in it. He see the opening! This is going to happen! “So…” he says, eyeing the ladies up & down, “let’s go over to my boat, I think I have a box of wine left from my last charter.”

Men just don’t get it.

Your boat does not impress me. I promise you. You need more than money and a boat to impress me. Besides, have you even watched the news lately? That is how people disappear! I am not stupid enough to go get on your boat, go out on the open sea and truly believe I am coming home unharmed. Now, I realize you may be perfectly safe. But I have no way of knowing that. I don’t think they hand out registration cards that say, “Certified Safe Guy” (Although there is an idea. Let me put some thought into that). Or conversely, I could be an axe murderer for all you know! Do you really want to be somewhere completely deserted with me if you cannot scream for help when you find out I am a raging psychopath? No? Well neither do I. On a side note; if I look at a wine list and can pick a glass without asking the bartender for a recommendation, a box will not impress me. Take your “Two-Buck-Chuck” out for some other special occasion; perhaps when your mom comes to visit you on your boat.

"The Next Level"

He has been friends with her for a long time. She is witty. The two of you engage in conversation almost daily. You both laugh, you both joke around, and most of all you both relate on almost every level. He can have a deep conversation with her about anything. She confesses her soul. She has cried on his shoulder. Obviously he has hit the "friend zone". One day, there is tension. Not argument tension but that sexual tension where he thinks something more might be said. She stands in front of him daring him to make a move. She must be joking. She tells you, "I will never make the first move, but when you do, I will not say no." She smiles wickedly. She leans over and you can see the swell of her breasts thru the low cut shirt she has on. She could not be serious. She is joking. He is SURE of it. He laughs and change the topic.

Men just don't get it.

Let me assure you, I am not kidding. I am giving you the golden egg. You win. But I will not move first, mostly because that is a man's job. Second, I am not 100% certain if you are willing to risk our friendship for some wild night. But I am telling you right now, I am. You will not regret it. Just jump off that ledge. In fact I dare you.

"Blunt"

There is a woman alone at the bar on a cruise ship, having a nice conversation with the bartender along with her glass of wine. He comes over to sit next to her & strikes up a conversation as the bartender takes his leave. He compliments her & she smiles. Then he leans in & whispers, "What's your room number? My wife is in the lounge over there watching the show but she'll be a little while longer, I really want to just do you right now."

Men just don't get it.

Really?! If this requires any explanation; please kindly send me your wife's contact information. Ah, who am I kidding – she already knows you're a complete schmuck; I don't need to tell her.

“Buying Drinks”

Walking through the casino in Vegas he spies a table at the champagne bar. Three enticing women with cocktails on the table in front of them are laughing. He saunters to bar and orders a drink. They have not noticed him… yet. Watching from the corner of his eye, he takes a sip of his drink, watching & waiting to see if any men are joining them. Once satisfied they are alone he begins his approach. He slides in next to the closest and introduces himself. He uses the winning line of, “So what are three beautiful ladies like you doing here alone?” They laugh, but he assumes it is because he is so charming. He invites them to his private table at the dance club. He is smooth so his lines get better. “So why would you three gorgeous creatures want to pay for drinks when I have a private booth with bar service in the hottest club in town? Lets go!” He is shocked when one looks him right in the eye and replies, “Why would I let you pay for my drinks?” The other two laugh mumbling about how he is in for it now. He is a little irritated his line that has always worked does not seem to have an effect! He responds tartly, “You are telling me, you would rather pay for drinks then take mine?” Of course this is not logical! He is completely sure he has won now. She replies, “Yes I would. Have fun in your booth.” He walks away confused and unaware of what just happened.

Men just don’t get it.

Maybe this is just me. Granted I have known many women who disagree. Their sole purpose is to go out and find unsuspecting fools to pay for drinks and then ignore them. Boys, pay attention to this part... They don't want you, just your wallet. I do not take a drink from a guy across the bar. That just allows him ownership for lack of a better term. If I want to talk to you, get to know you, maybe spend the night with you; trust me you will know. Then buy me a drink. Don't think simply because you sent it from across the bar I am now beholden to talk to you all night because I won't. I will save you that $10 right now. And if you send it to me anyway? Do not be surprised if the server brings it right back to you.

“Dumb & Dumber”

Act 1: He and his friend spy a couple of cute girls in a bar, dancing & enjoying themselves. They are making friends along the way & having fun. He makes eye contact & they are dancing his way. He is grinning ear to ear; his buddy is thrilled, too! Good work friend! All is fun & dancing continues – until his friend leans in and whispers into one of the girls ear, “I’m gonna find you tonight.”

Act 2: He is somehow able to get the other girl’s phone number, even talk to her once & are actually a bit charming. Then… his first text message the next day, oh yes, this will get her attention! Oh yes, she will love this! She is at work in a meeting & voila! …A photo of him jacking off.

Men REALLY just don’t get it.

Ok, Mr. Act 1 - so we have said we like a man who takes control. Just don’t try to do it in the first hour we have met you! Again, this changes things from ‘man’ to ‘crazy stalker’.

… and for Mr. Act 2 – this is NOT what a woman wants to see from you after speaking to you only a couple of times. Save that for your long term girlfriend, wife or whatever… or send it to your hooker! This is not a turn on.

"The Family Friend"

He is a friend of the family. He has flirted with her forever it seems. He sees her constantly. He wants her, she wants him. It is obvious by the smoldering fire throughout both of their bodies when they see each other. Sexual innuendos are the only banter they share. She tells him, "I broke up my boyfriend and need some attention. Know where I could find some?" He suggests a popular online dating site to her. There is no way her Dad would approve of this.

Men just don't get it.

Why do you do this to me? You know I want you. There is no doubt you would be interested as well. I realize you have other complications, but seriously you are killing me here buddy. When does it get to be the time when I simply say, put up or shut up?

<u>"Sending in the Estrogen"</u>

He is the bartender and part owner of the local bar. Girls are always are flirting with him. He is hot, yet he does not really know it. He has no interest in any of them until one night this dark haired temptress walked in the door. She is there with a friend and he feels something. A smoldering in the pit of his stomach as she looks him directly in the eye and smiles. She is daring him to make a move. Let the game begin! It has been awhile since he was interested and he is a little rusty. She is quick and slows down her game to let him be comfortable and catch up. His best female friend notices. She is thrilled because he has not shown interest in anyone in a long time. She follows this beauty into the restroom. She proceeds to start a conversation while applying lip gloss. "He is my best friend, and has been for years. He is so focused on the business he does not have time to date. I have never seen him interested in anyone walking in the door! Consider yourself very fortunate. He is an amazing guy!"

Men just don't get it.

Ok I don't know if you sent her in to talk to me or not, but this is the moment I left. To all you men out there with female friends, she either wants you for herself or didn't like me for whatever reason. I can hear you all shouting out there how can that possibly be true? She was helping! She was talking me up! Actually no she was not. I have known you for a little more than an hour. You are working so there has not even been a conversation yet! Did I walk in the bar with a sign on my forehead that said, "I want a relationship with an amazing guy and his best friend!"? I don't think I did. Do yourself a favor and ask out your friend. She wants to have a relationship with you. Don't believe me? I will bet you $100 right now if you ask her out she is going to say yes.

<u>"Sudden Death"</u>

He is enjoying some time in the dance club with his friends aboard a weekend getaway cruise. He sees that the line at the bar is too long to wait so he decides to walk to the cigar bar to get a drink & take a break from the 'scene'. As he orders a cocktail, she approaches. You make some small talk & have her laughing before long. While not her typical 'type', she is enjoying the chatter. As she turns to head back to the club, he hands her his business card, winks at her & say, "Give me a call!" She is walking back into the club when she reads his card. She almost falls on the floor laughing. Her friends are quizzing her as to what's so funny. She throws his card at them & they pick it up – before long they are in hysterics, too. You are a mortician!

Men just don't get it.

We all have to make a living. Fine. It's not about what you do. Let me fill you in on the first thing a woman thinks about when you hand her your 'mortician' card at a first meeting. At this point, there's nothing but thoughts of embalming & where your hands have been that are now running through her head. Ewwww! So listen up all of you embalmers, morticians, garbage men, sewer workers, medical examiners, proctologists, slaughter house owners & guano collectors; take it from me – if you have one of 'those' jobs; save the business card. Don't go <u>there</u> if you wanna go <u>there</u>. Get the drift?

Chapter 2: Thanks, But No Thanks

For every clueless man with a worthless pick-up line you get the guy who runs a decent game. Sometimes it is one last slip up in the end that will send us girls running the other direction. Ever wonder what it was? Well here you go! Some classic slip-ups that ruined what was going great!!

"Taking Initiative"

He is at the bar. A cute girl is next to him. He strikes up conversation. She is obviously flirting. She likes him! The closer he looks the more attracted he is. After a half an hour or so of obvious attraction and random flirting, he excuses himself. Perfect! She has time to let her friends know about him, powder her nose, and refresh lip gloss. He joins his friends across the bar. She is watching him. She is smiling. It is game on for sure. As closing time inches closer he finds his way back. And he chats. And chats. And chats…….. She kisses him on the cheek and says good night. He got a number, but she doesn't return the calls. What happened?

Men just don't get it.

Wow you had her. All you had to do was take her by the hand and tell her where you both were going next. She is not gonna do that for you buddy. Fatal flaw, not taking the initiative! I cannot tell you how many times I have sat there and talked to you, whoever you are until I get in my car/wander back to my room alone. TELL ME WHAT YOU WANT. That is the biggest turn on of all.

“The L word”

He finally meets up & gets the “date” with the girl he has been seeing around the office. They go out, have fun, dance… even make plans to meet up again next week and again the week after. So, for their third date in as many weeks – he decides it’s time to tell her, “I love you!” She began avoiding him at the office, not taking his calls & when he finally does get in touch with her, she declines any further dates.

Men just don’t get it.

Although many guys believe this is the way to a woman’s heart – that is pure BS! Pushing things too far too fast & use of the “L” word are serious no-nos. Save that crap for your mommy until we’ve been seriously dating several months.

<u>“Bitchy Wife”</u>

He and his friends are on a cruise. They are all dressed up in suits ready for dinner. This woman in a short black dress comes up to him and tells him seeing a good looking man in a suit and a tie is <u>so hot</u>. It reminds her of opening presents. She asks if he is <u>her</u> present. Now the two of them have been making eye contact for days. She smiles and runs her hands up and down the buttons of his shirt. She says maybe I will see him later, smiles and walks away. Wow! His buddies’ jaws are on the floor. He feels like this could not have possibly happened. Fast forward to after dinner. She is leaning on the bar smoking a cigarette. He walks up to her and say, “Smoking is disgusting you know.” She taps him on the nose and says, “It could have been fun!” as she saunters away.

Men just don’t get it.

Look, you do not have to approve of what I do; if you do not like it that is fine. Don’t call me out on it. You are not my mother, and we have just met. Trust me I have kissed enough boys to know when I need to run to the room and brush my teeth and chew gum. I understand smoking tastes gross to you. I will fix it though. Too bad... What a loss. He was cute too! Unfortunately after that I did refer to you as the “Bitchy Wife” the rest of the cruise. Sorry!

<u>"Tantrums"</u>

He can sing to her all night; she knows it's like this all the time. Eyes locked & his voice is so sweet. She has got his number, but she does not care – She might actually like him anyway. It's been days of flirting & his sexy smile have grown on her. He shuts down a bit early tonight & comes over to talk to her and her friends. Just when she thinks she may ask him if he would like to take a walk, woops – someone across the room touched his guitar. His temper flares hotter than necessary & he turns around to berate the offender. He turns back toward her but she is already gone.

Men just don't get it.

Temper tantrums are not sexy. Period.

<u>“The Threesome”</u>

He has been talking to her friend. The girls are out together so she knows who he is. He laughs and jokes with her, while he uses some of his best moves on her friend. She likes him. They all hang out. She runs from here to there, making friends while her friend stays close to him using her best flirting right back. She comes back whisper a joke to her friend, they laugh, they hug, they dance, maybe even peck each other on the cheek. He thinks he will have her. But then a stroke of brilliance hits him. This could be it. Every man’s fantasy! He WILL have them both! He slyly states that he would be game. He receives looks of annoyance and they both leave. What happened?

Men just don’t get it.

Ok gentlemen we are here to tell you the truth. We don’t have pillow fights in lingerie and we don’t make out with each when you leave. We are sorry to burst your bubble. Let us tell you what we <u>will</u> do so you can distinguish the difference. Close girlfriends love each other. In a way you could not possibly understand. We hug, we dance close, we trade clothes, we peck each other’s cheeks, we call each other beautiful etc. At any given point while we are getting ready we may decide to trade blouses and we will get naked in front of each other for that. But not sex. We repeat this does not mean sex. We know it is hard to believe that we can keep our hands off of each other as soon as the door closes, but somehow we manage.

<u>"Keeping In Touch"</u>

He's beautiful to look at. She watches him play basketball and when he pulls off his shirt she confirms that he is one sexy man. Cut in all the right places and glistening in sweat he gets the girl feeling all tingly inside. He approaches & says "Hi!". By his tone, she knows that perhaps later they will meet again for midnight rendezvous. Several times through the week they enjoy the hook up, he is her vacation tryst. He knows what he is doing both on and off the basketball court. As the final day of vacation nears, he tells her how much he will miss not seeing her every day when they return to their regular lives. He insists that they keep in touch.

Men just don't get it.

Now I know you must be thinking - how can this man only almost get it? You didn't call or write me an email! Now do not be fooled into thinking I had any belief this was going to turn into some whirlwind romance and we were going to live happily ever after. I know that is not the case. But why fake it? I was on vacation too, you big beautiful dork. Don't ask for contact information if you are not going to use it. It just makes both of us look dumb. All I wanted was to drop you a note to say how "nice" it was to have met you and thank you for a good time. Now I just think you are a tool.

“Baggage Claim”

Ahhh, he’s such a little quirky nerd. Yes, he’s adorable, tall & blonde, with boyish charm & a twinkle in his eye. She laughs at his jokes when they meey and enjoys some good times on that weekend getaway. She actually seems to have a lot in common with him & enjoys his company - talking & flirting endlessly. Yes, she was having fun until that night. That night when she asked her roommate to stay out a bit later so they could have some time alone. The night that could have been magical… if only he could have focused on enjoying her & the moment, instead of flashing back in time to old memories. Crying and telling her about his first sexual experience. Crying & asking about hers. Yep… he is the guy who’s just a bit f*&^! up. Sorry; she feels bad for him – she really does, but she’s only known him for a few days & this is his baggage. She is not going to be his baggage handler.

Men just don’t get it.

Ok, we’ve got it. We all have baggage; some of us much more than others; some of us much worse than others. Now, this is not a deal breaker in the long term & light “carry on” baggage is generally ok if we really like you... but PLEASE, guys, please, don’t lay your deepest darkest secrets on us after only a few days & most definitely not just as you’re about to get lucky. This behavior will have us running for the hills.

"Showtime!"

Well hello to you Mr. Suit. Yes, my friends still call him the "Art Boy". He ran an art gallery and took me for a private tour. I have always had a passion for art and he impressed me with his knowledge. How could I resist him? Tall, wavy dark hair & a look in his eye that said, "Let's go!" He had an adorable smile and eyes that undressed me instantly. I could feel the heat between us the moment we met on the dance floor. He kissed me with a passion that melted my knees and gave me butterflies in my stomach. Believe me I knew it was not serious. But I definitely had a crush.

Men just don't get it!

Why do men think once we sleep together I will be the crazy stalker? Are women really like this or do we just have a bad reputation? You did not have to bring in another girl the next night to scare me off. I wouldn't have left my friends the moment you walked in the room and glued myself to your side. Don't ruin a good thing by running scared the next day and taking preventative measures before you even see what is going to happen. I did have a good laugh at you when you walked in with the other woman and made a show of being in deep conversation with her until you left. It was obviously a show. But you didn't need to perform for my benefit.

Chapter 3: YES, Please!

We must take a moment to clarify the title of this chapter. Please remember, gentlemen, the following must be taken in line with the context of the subject matter of this book: flings, short term romances, vacation trysts, and maybe – just maybe the beginning of something new & fun. When we refer to "Men Who Got It"… we are not referring to relationships. We are not referring to even men we have communicated with after the affair. We are simply outlining the right way to come into (and leave) a chance meeting in a way which leaves everyone smiling & feeling good about the encounter for whatever it was. Whether the romance is continued or not is up to you, but learning from these guys should give you a leg up on the competition!

"Hook, Line & Sinker"

I saw you this morning. I looked over the heads of everyone in the room and gave you a slow, smoldering smile. You smiled back as you looked me up and down. You knew I appreciated looking and acknowledged it. You are with your friends and I am with mine but we are at the same event all day. I will catch up with you later and you confirm that in your open stare. Never speaking but all day I catch you looking as I am looking right back. Confidence is oozing out of your every pore. I play flirt with other men and you speak to other women throughout the day and evening knowing full well by the end of the night you will be mine. The event is winding down. You slowly mingle about the room moving closer until you are speaking to a group of men next to me. The woman I am talking to notices. She makes an attempt to stop what is going on to hopefully win the prize herself. She says to me, "Are you and the man you were talking to earlier together? You make a cute couple!" You speak up and turn the heads of everyone around us. "She has much bigger fish to fry tonight than that little boy." I look you directly in the eye and smile. The crowd fades out. You take me by the hand and lead me upstairs to your room without another word said.

This man got it!

Oh wow reliving this through writing reminds me again of how exactly hot this was. You were in control and were so ... a man. You made me feel like the most attractive woman alive and I made you feel like a man that night. Did we ever talk again? Nope, but what a night! Thank you Hottie Mc Hot!

<u>"Tell It Like It Is"</u>

Finally, you have a weekend away with your buddies. You know it's going to be a great one. It's your first evening out with your crew & you know you're out to play. You spy them. Three sexy girls. The eye contact starts & the flirting begins. One of the girls takes a dare, comes to your group of friends & asks if she & her friends can take a picture with all of you because you guys are hot. You volunteer your lap for her & photos are taken. The night wears on & we all dance together. You can't quite read the one you're after. She tends to ebb & flow; on & off of the dance floor. Never quite giving you the 'go'. Fast forward to the next day, you see her again. She's with her friends & you're with some of yours – but some have paired off with others. You play your game, she plays hers & you click. Driving each other mad & up a wall with hot intensity by never really putting it all out there. Finally, there's a dare. You tell her what you want. You tell her that she's driving you crazy. She gets that gleam in her eye, takes you by the hand, kisses you & says, "You can't read me? Then I'll just have to show you what I'm thinking." … and she does.

This man got it!

Oh young 'J' man, you were a charm & I'm still in awe of your strength. Playing the game of the flirt & simply showing how entranced you were, without ever pushing it. Eye contact, boys… Build the fire one log at a time & it will burn so hot. This, too, was a one night thing; no phone numbers exchanged or false promises. Take note, there were no regrets for anyone – just a really fun memory for the road.

"Feelin Sexy"

We are working together for the weekend out of town. You accidentally brush against me as I am filling our trade show booth with various media pamphlets and samples. As I speak to people you watch me across the room giving me the sexiest smile. When you speak to me, it is barely a whisper so I have to lean in close to hear you. We had worked together before but never just the two of us. As the evening wraps up I feel the fire smoldering between us. You suggested meeting at the hotel bar for a drink. It is obvious you have more in mind. You have my favorite drink waiting for me when I arrive and your southern drawl and manners make me tingle inside. You interrupt me while I am discussing the day's events. You lean in close to my ear and I can feel your breathe on me. You say, "You are the sexiest woman in the room. Every man at the bar is envious of me sitting here with you and all their eyes are on us. Watching you all day has been driving me insane. Let me take you upstairs now and have my way with you." We quickly pay the bill and go to your room.

This man got it, too!

With the right compliment you can drive any woman mad. It makes her feel sexy and in return she will be putty in your hands. Every time we traveled together after this we had midnight rendezvous' and I always looked forward to it. You were extremely attentive in and out of the bedroom. And you always walked me to my door. Southern Gentleman charm will make me weak in the knees every time! Oh and that accent? Wow...

“Handcuffs, I Hate You”

Ahh, the first evening of a weeklong getaway aboard a fabulous ship at the casino bar, and I would look forward to that spot every day. Truth be told, I still don’t even know how you initially came to be part of the commotion that first night. I was a pretty busy gal, dancing & making friends with everyone. It was the moment you showed me the way to the ladies room & took that opportunity to tell me that you were interested & then steal a sweet kiss. You had my number right from the start & never let me get away with a thing. Smart move. It was the twinkle in your eye & your willingness to put up with the plethora of our antics that got you through. Subtle confidence & wit was the key. You were not part of the plan. My game was thrown. I told you time & time again – “You’re too real for this”. “I hate you”. “I never want to see you again”. You laughed & responded, “I hate you, too. See you tomorrow.” You’re a real man with charms all your own & yet you are as playful as I in your own way. From day 1, you played it right & had the other men around in jaw dropping awe of your ‘in’. Your nickname (Handcuffs) came from other groups of men, not from Alice or Lucille… it was others who saw us all singing, dancing, & playing - out & about together. What a magnificent week it was.

This man really got it!

Gentlemen, take note – humor & wit go a long way. If you want to be in the mix, you must become friendly (but not too friendly) with your target’s friends. Go with the flow. Never make her feel like she has to depart from her friends or who she is to spend some time with you – at least before it’s time to take her home for some ‘one-on-one fun’. Our “Cop” & inspiration for this book understood this well. I will never forget that week. I will never forget our balcony escapades. I will never forget his laugh. I will never forget his smell. I will never forget the way he looked at me. I will never forget his hands in my hair. He’s the one the boys call “Handcuffs”. I hate him. I never want to see him again. So, how did this one end? This one is…to be continued for maybe just one more weekend tryst.

****If I can just chime in here for a moment, I happened to be the friend when we met Mr. Handcuffs. Let me just say you are awesome. You never made me feel like the third wheel while the two of you were connecting. You talked to me as much as you talked to her. It was entirely refreshing to meet a man who knew how to play the game as well as you do. You never made the fatal flaw, hinting about the threesome. You pointed out hot guys (And not so hot guys, I might never forgive you for the "Camp Counselor" comments) to me all the while working quite the impact on my dear friend. Let me give you a standing ovation at this one. You are the first man I have ever met who knew how to handle this situation to perfection.*

Chapter 4: The 'Cougar' Label

Alice's Perspective:

I think it is time to move on to a little personal commentary concerning the term "Cougar". This year on a couple occasions I have heard this term jokingly reflected to me. At first I was offended. In my head I conjure up pictures of a haggard old woman with too much fake and bake tanning and bad plastic surgery chasing 21 year old boys who are looking for a paycheck. You know the ones I am taking about yes? You see them at your local gym or neighborhood bar. You laugh and wonder how they can possibly even aspire to get these cute young boys. For instance, at my local bar there are several regulars. They wear their corsets and cheap imitation leather miniskirts with panty hose so you cannot see the wrinkles in their legs. If they cannot afford plastic surgery they literally tape back the wrinkles around their face and wear their bleach blond hair long and straggly to cover it. They look like early 1980's version of Madonna except in a scary variation. (As a side note to my dear friend Lucille, if I ever try to pull off this look please slap me and send me to the nursing home for dementia related issues).

I am not bragging to say I look pretty good for my age as does Lucille. We are frequently met with surprise when we reveal how old we truly are. I am neither a hard core workout fiend nor a diet Nazi. I simple pay attention and when something fits a little too tight I watch what I eat. (Beer unfortunately is my downfall. Ahh the sweet nectar of the gods is not kind to my waist line). I walk my dog every day and try to be somewhat active. Here in lies the problem. I can and do still chase the mid-twenty something boys and get chased right back. They are pretty to look at and even more fun to play with. Whoever said women reach their sexual peak in thier mid-thirties was not lying. I am divorced and have no interest in giving up all the fun I am having with being single at this time. Most men my age are looking for a relationship. I am not. Maybe someday, but I am just having too much damn fun right now.

Upon further thought though, this title of "Cougar" needs to have a face lift as much as the old cronies at the bar. And what really constitutes a cougar? Do you have to be over 40 to gain this crown? Or is it simply chasing boys 15 years younger than me? If this is the case then I am not a cougar yet! (Wheeewww dodged that bullet!) But if Cougar only means I like to spend time with younger men, then count me in and I will wear it proudly. This is not to say I am only looking for younger men. If you are pretty to look at, can have a witty conversation and don't want to marry me and have kids we will get along just fine. Now if you are younger fair warning. I am not going to pay your bills or support you through college or whatever else goes along with dating cougars. Just thought I should throw that out there! I guess I should also mention that if you are older, I do not want to raise your children, clean your house, or be in your bridge club. Lucille, your thoughts?

Lucille weighs in:

I am not a "Cougar". To this day, I detest that label. I have considered myself simply as a MILF (for those yet uneducated on the acronym – Mom I'd Like to F&*%) since I learned that term several years ago. Most young men will guess my age as somewhere between 27-30; if that's their guess then I tell them they are correct. Who am I to argue? I will also admit I have been called Mrs. Robinson twice after revealing my true age – which is amusing in itself, in that the word has always been used only by the boys who had something to prove in the way of them *not* needing a teacher themselves. (If this was you – you're 50/50 in being correct on that one, I'll let you guess which 50%!)

"MILF", "Mrs. Robinson", "Cougar"… I'm not entirely sure which is the least evil of the terms.

My mind is - like Alice's - is slowly changing & evolving. In fact, I was recently informed that one can be a MILF and a "Cougar" at the same time. Of course, when I cringed at the notion, that statement was quickly clarified by the gentleman that "Cougars" must be over 40, which I am not. (I must also note that he was worried about becoming a scene in Chapter 1 of this book at the time & he was careful to note the claw marks as coming from a jaguar after that evening, rather than a cougar.) I digress…

So, this is the new era of dating for fun & not for the necessary procreation of the population. As we evolve though the terms we place on this generation (MY generation) of single women who have either completed their role as wife or never chose to play it at all; I must agree that if the world is ready to brand all single women in their 30's or 40's who play with, flirt with or take home boys in their 20's as "Cougars", then I will begin to work on embracing the term. Although, not without a great big "Thank You" to Courtney Cox & her role on the sitcom Cougar Town[1]

---

[1] *Cougar Town*. Executive Producers: David Arquette, Courteney Cox, Bill Lawrence, Kevin Biegel; ABC Television, 2009.

for paving the way to rebranding the word. (The woman is hot, I don't care who ya are & her wardrobe is amazing!)

And for one final thought before we fully decide what the word "cougar" means to our generation's place in time; what do we call the men in their 30's and 40's or even 50s who date women in their 20s or 30s? Oh yes… that's right. They are branded "Lucky", "Smart", "Smooth" or "Rich".

Chapter 5: The Workout

Alice's Perspective:

I think it is worth noting a bit about the workout. Have you ever had wild, hanging from the chandelier, acrobatic sex? You know what I mean then. Up against walls, over balcony railings and half propped up on various furniture pieces. This is FUN. Do not think that for a minute I am putting this down. Wild out of control sex can be and is fantastic. However, sometimes doesn't that big cushy bed look nice? I recently met a man that must have thought I was a contortionist. I guess I set a standard that first night. It was fun and sexy. I woke up the next morning smiling from ear to ear with every muscle in my body sore. I felt like I had spent three hours working out with weights in the gym. If I am propping myself up, I am also holding up your weight. Now depending on how long this goes on it can turn into the equivalent of doing hundreds of push-ups.

Two days later, when we ended up back in my room once again it was wild. We never touched a bed once. Everywhere around the bed and on the balcony but by the time he left, my bed was still made without even a wrinkle in the bedspread. I tried to direct it that way several times but you knew what you liked and damn you were good at it so who was I to complain? In the morning I woke up with every muscle in my body screaming at me. I felt like before we had sex again I need six months of massive boot camp training. My muscles burned so bad I thought I had been in a prizefight! I was just beat up. Lucille laughed at me because I could not even raise my arms over my head to put on a shirt. I must apologize to you for blowing you off the last two nights of vacation and just going to bed by myself but I was sure if there was another night like that so close together I might die. Yes, as ridiculous as it sounds I am complaining about great sex. It was great but sometimes a girl just likes to be on her back or see you on your back.

Along those same lines let's talk about how long it should last. Now I know for most of men's sexually active lives you hear all this advice such as, think about baseball, stop for a minute to regroup, and various other ways to make the moment last longer. This is not a marathon. Don't stop as I am about to get what I want so you can regroup. You kill it for me. A good fifteen or twenty minutes is great. We can do it again in an hour. And an hour after that and an hour after that if you are up to it. Don't ruin a great thing by trying to last for hours at a time. I realize this might be opposite of what you may of heard from all sources of advice but really. I don't want to be so sore I cannot walk tomorrow and you don't really want to separate yourself from the situation by thinking about baseball that you forget to enjoy yourself. It is not about length of time, it is about quality. There is nothing better than that magical moment happening at the same time. If it took 10 minutes or an hour I guarantee I will be just as happy with your performance.

Lucille weighs in:

Yet again, Alice & I agree on this one. We've all had a little lovin' the shower, windowsill, on the balcony, on the table, on top of the counters, in stairwells, in public laundry rooms, on children's play structures at midnight, in glass elevators, back seats of vehicles, park benches, showers, swimming pools, saunas, vending machine rooms, stadium seats, all sorts of floors, storage closets, restaurant booths, etc… Oh wait – you mean you haven't? Ok… well then, when you do – you'll realize it's not all it's cracked up to be. Fun? Yes. Satisfying? Not so much.

These escapades are certainly a challenge & as such are enjoyable in & of themselves. With that said, however, if I were to try to attempt all of the above on consecutive nights (ok, there was that one week in Seattle) I know that I would not be so adventurous. We know that you think that you have to do a majority of the work. As Alice points out in her notes, we have to bear your weight as well as our own. This can be quite a challenge. In those cases where we may not be bearing your weight – our knees are scrapping concrete or are getting splinters. We end up with nasty bruises on our rear ends (or other places). This all makes the next day just plain hurt.

I say – play it up. Just do it one at a time & if you have the ability to move it to that soft cushy bed – do your lady a favor & save her some pain. Who knows, you may even save yourself a few battle wounds in the process. Of course, then you wouldn't have the scars to show off to your buddies, but I guarantee that when we're feeling good & sexy – you come out the winner.

Moving on to the subject of 'time'. Screw baseball, football, your mom's face or whatever other tactics you have seen in the movies. Alice is 100% on the mark. If it's a problem to last long enough for me, we'll go again. I have faith that you're not going to leave me hangin'. One way or another (there are, after all,

LOTS of ways) you can ensure my satisfaction without the marathon.

Chapter 6: Communication in the Afterglow

Lucille's perspective:

You: "Can I get your number? Maybe we can hook up again sometime!"

Me: "Sorry, I'm just not that kind of girl."

You: "You're not what kind of girl?"

Me: "The kind that wants to give you her phone number."

Yes, this is a verbatim conversation I had with a boy after the 'hook up'.

You will note that in chapters 2 & 3, the Men Who Just Might Get It & the Men Who Got It, there are several references to things going well up & until 'after' the hook up. It seems there are no set boundaries for you guys on how, if or when you should communicate with a girl after the deed is done. We have all heard about the "Three Day Rule". We have all heard the advice that you want to play it 'cool' in the first days after meeting someone. Certainly, it's not a cut & dry situation, but how you approach her in day or two after your encounter will certainly determine whether or not there might be a second meeting – or if she will decide to not respond. I'm telling you now; if she actually gave you her contact information you are being given the go-ahead to use it. If we didn't want to give it to you, we wouldn't have.

At this point, if you have decided to contact her at all – you have made some kind of determination in your own mind of what you're after. Perhaps it's subconscious. Perhaps your mom taught you to be a 'good boy'. Perhaps you really like her. Perhaps you're even in the market for a relationship. I'm telling you now – before you make that phone call or send that email, you need to determine if you are just looking for another hook up or if you want to get to know her better. The timing of your approach & her response to you will depend on you knowing what you want! Once you have made up your mind in that regard, you will know what method to use to contact her & when.

"The Three Day Rule"… UGH - so passé. You have heard that if you really like her, you need to wait three days to contact her or she won't respect you. I'm here to tell you that this is BS. The three day rule should be used if & only if you are interested in nothing more than another meet up for a hook up. See, here's the deal. If she really liked you & had even considered for a second that she might go out with you again to get to know you on another level – you have 36 hours to contact her. Period. After that, she is writing you off as a fun fling. Likewise, if you had given her your contact information, you will be able to tell where she stands by this same 'new rule'. Within 36 hours – she likes you. More than that – sorry buddy, you're out; though you could make the list of second hook ups if her schedule permits. Believe me, though, you won't be at the top of it.

The other issue that comes up all the time is, to call or to email? Obviously, whatever contact info she gave you is a start. Let me fill you in on this one; if she gave you only her email address – this is both a defensive measure & a *test*. This allows her to detach a bit, just in case you don't contact her while giving her time to analyze your message when it does come in so that she can respond appropriately (and within 24 hours if she likes you, more if she's unsure)... and then the *test* – do you ask for her phone #?

Alice Weighs In:

I agree with Lucille whole heartedly on this one. I am not one to beat around the bush. If I gave you my contact information (By the way always email for me, and not my work email. Always personal) then I want you to contact me. If we are lying there in the "afterglow" and you ask me if you will see me again and I say no, don't get offended please. Simply take it as a fun night and move on.

Also, important to note, I won't ask you for yours either. This is basically my way of finding out if you wanted to go any further with this. I will walk out of the room with a smile on my face without contact information every time if you don't ask for mine even if I would like to see you again. Why? Maybe I have a slight touch of old fashion in me where it is the boy's job to ask girls out. Now I realize that probably sounds like the biggest oxymoron you have ever heard having now read these 5 chapters of the book. Feel free to laugh at me for this contradiction. Believe me I am. But I am still a woman and it is a woman's prerogative to be silly and not make sense sometimes right?

Email and texting make it so convenient to carefully think out what I want to say. I will be honest and tell you I am a phone commando. I speak to the point of why I called and get off. Unless you can fill the silence with chit chat that I can respond to, you will find yourself off the phone with me fast. But, email and texting I will do all day and all night long. This is another reason I only hand out email.

Within 48 hours of parting ways if I have not heard from you, I am over it. If I am excited about meeting you, and interested in speaking to you some more and getting to know you, I want you to be excited about it as well. If you are not, oh well. If I choose to put any sort of effort getting to know you, then you better exert the same level of enthusiasm. I have been around the block a couple times and realize it is a waste of both of our times if we are not on the same page in this regard.

Now if you are simply looking for someone to send that midnight rendezvous text to, maybe we can arrange that as well.

One further item to note; In today's world of social networking, a lot of personal information is floating around out there in cyberspace. Do me one favor. Don't send me a friend request from your favorite website out there without emailing me first PLEASE? I realize once again it is a contradicting, being a private person and having public profiles, but if I "friend" you on these websites, I am letting you climb into a window of my life. If you lost my email or cell number, and you find me on the site, use the private message to let me know. Don't just send me a friend request without a note. I will probably hit the "quietly ignore" button because I feel like you are snooping! To me, it is almost akin to peeping in my windows to see what I do every day. (Of course if you are out there looking in my windows, **I know about it**, and I like you, you might get a little show for fun).

Chapter 7: Manners, Get Some If You Want Some

I am sure like all good mothers do for their boys, you were taught to open doors, pull out chairs, and use good manners. Believe me, we do appreciate it. I know you hear a lot of the "I can do it myself" type attitudes these days. I CAN do it myself but that does not mean I want to! Good manners are worth bonus points! Bonus points can be redeemed for some very fun things!

1. Opening Car Doors

This is not a requirement, but if you want to get into 'the door', we'd advise you to open the car door for us.

2. Bringing Flowers

Once again, not required, but I like flowers. I have heard a lot of girls say I don't like them, they just die. Then they get them, and they cannot wait to tell all their friends just how sweet you are. If you know my favorites, that is additional points for you. Side note to that though – Do not send them to my work. That is laying a claim to everyone in the office that I have a "boyfriend" and am off limits. Not a good approach in a new friendship.

3. Presents

A man I met recently referred to me as the girl who likes presents. I found this funny but let me explain myself. I don't care if you spent $1 or $1,000,000. If you see a little something you know I will love bring it to me. I will be happy and I can tell you 99.9% of the time you will get lucky. Need an example? When I was a kid I loved a certain board game. The next time my ex-boyfriend saw me after I had told him that, he had it for me all wrapped up in a bow. We never did make it out that night and I changed to the rules to involve stripping. Everybody wins!

4. Timeliness

Nothing is worse than a man (or anyone for that matter) who thinks they are too good to be when & where they say they will be. Ok, sometimes things happen & we are delayed. Fine. Use your communication device. There's no excuse in the age of mobile communication to just leave someone else waiting on you. Once you may be able to get away with. Twice? Buh-Bye! You're just not worth my time.

5. Dress for Success

On average your typical woman who is getting ready to go out is going to take at least an hour and change her clothes a minimum of twice. If she is going to see you and she is into you, that will double in both aspects. I know it will not take you that long to get ready, but put some thought into what is covering your body. If you look good I will spend the time we are together trying to figure out how to take it off of you. If you show up in a tailored suit that fits you right? We are not going anywhere for awhile. <u>That is just too sexy not to rip it off of you.</u>

6. Cologne

If I wake up in the morning and can smell your scent on my pillow, in my skin and through my hair, I will be thinking about calling you to come over to go back to bed. There is just nothing like good cologne on a man. If you do not know what to buy, go to your local department store. Ask the salesgirl at the counter to help you pick (all colognes smell different once applied to YOUR skin) and let her show you how much to use. That is very important. I know you have walked by that guy on the street that smells like they bathed in cologne. Your eyes water and nostrils burn when you get within three feet of them. Do not fall into this trap! If I cannot get close to you without feeling like I was just hit with tear gas you are not going to get your hands on me.

7. Your Place

We don't expect it to be white glove clean. We know you are busy, we know not everyone has a maid to get into the bitty gritty & clean all day. Heck, even my place could use a once over. There is, however, one area you MUST keep reasonably cleaned up if you are having a gal over to you place. The bathroom, guys, the BATHROOM! Do I need to say it again? Clean up the BATHROOM before she arrives! I guarantee she will be using it & there is nothing grosser than pee all over the seat & razor stubble in the sink.

8. Your "Raincoat"

I always try and carry protection with me when I go out as should you. Sometimes moments "spring" up when you least expect it. Between the two of us we should have it covered, no pun intended. Don't ruin the moment for me by trying to talk me into trusting you because you trust me. Trust me? You do not even know me! I cannot even imagine you wanting to take that risk with someone you only met a few days ago (Ok, ok, maybe a few hours ago). I don't trust you and if I have to flat out say it I am leaving because you have simply spoiled my mood. This is not up for discussion on the first date. (Ok! Maybe it wasn't even technically a "date").

Chapter 8: The Perfect Flirt

This chapter is just a reflection of those perfect little moments in time, where there was no opportunity to go any further than a quick flirt; an ego boost. From our perspective, these men did it just right. We had smiles on our faces the rest of the day. If we could get this every morning we're certain that the world would be a better place.

"Coffee"

I enter the local coffee house with one eye open. I am not sure why I am so tired this morning. It is just going to be one of those days. I order my cup of coffee and sit and wait for them to pour it. You are on your laptop at a table near the door. You look over and smile. As I unsuccessfully try to stifle a yawn, you laugh and ask me, "It looks like an extra shot of espresso morning for you. Long night?" I laugh and you introduce yourself. We chat for a minute. I would have never noticed you before. You are not my type but you suddenly were cuter than I originally thought. I get my coffee and get ready to leave. You tell me I look pretty and you hope I have a good day as I walk out the door. I am awake now! That was a nice way to wake up and I am ready for the day.

"Banking"

I head over to handle some business at the bank. You have been my teller a few times. When I walk up to the counter this morning, you smile big and remember my name. You ask me about work as we handle my business. You are adorable but I never really noticed. With a twinkle in your eye and a big smile you tell me as I am leaving, "I hope you are dating someone, because your smile is fantastic and someone deserves to see that every morning." I blushed. Now I don't think I have actually blushed and been flustered like that in YEARS. I thank you and leave. I find myself looking forward to banking day now! I will not be going out or hooking up with my bank teller, but I smiled all day long thinking about him!

"The Office"

The flirt at work. We all have one of these. Even if it's just a friend or someone we rarely see around the office. Especially when it's someone we know we would never 'hook up' with nor 'date', this is the perfect flirt! There's one boy I always look forward to having meetings with. He looks at me & smiles – his eyes twinkle & crinkle up at the corners; I suddenly turn into a giggly little school girl. Here I am discussing all things practical with a grin on my face from ear to ear & butterflies in my stomach. He's just so cute! Advice to you boys… enjoy the flirt at work! It doesn't have to be any more than that (and never cross over into harassment, make sure it's subtle, light & reciprocated!) There's no better way to make someone's day!

"Traffic"

Drive time! Use it wisely! There is no better rush than getting 'eyed' while I drive home from work. You know the kind of 'eyeing' I mean. It's the neck craning, mock whistling, "Yow Baby" flirting from your car as we pass each other on our way home after a hard day. Just pick your target & do it! Pick many targets every day! Side note… flirting as you pass = good! Following her home or anywhere = BAD! We love the flirting – but most women will not appreciate you becoming crazy stalker guy.

"Single Dad"

Hello to the single dad. I see you at our kids functions. Whether it be little league, football practice, piano recitals, marching band car wash, or various other fundraising activities the game is always the same. The eye contact, the banter, the smile when I arrive. You don't want me to raise your kids anymore than I want you to raise mine. But when we are working closely together in the tiny snack bar there is heat and not just from the popcorn machine. All the married guys are jealous and all the wives hate us. I'll see you at practice tomorrow….

"The Market"

The grocery store is always fun for a flirt. Where else can you ask a woman about her melons or suggest the perfect cut of meat without getting slapped? Seriously, gents; the grocery store is another great place to enjoy the flirt of the moment! Pass her by & smile. Look her up & down. Wink at her across the checkout line or at the deli counter. Everyday chores can be so much more fun that way!

"Sports"

Our personal favorite flirt of all! The sporting event flirt! We prefer football. There is nothing like everyone tailgating, drinking beer, and decked out in their favorite teams gear. Let me give you a hint here. If your target is a fan of the same team as you, you already have an in. Don't be the obnoxious shirtless drunk guy with your tummy painted but be enthusiastic! If you are a true fan this is not a problem at all! You will share ups and downs, highs and lows. Lots of acceptable random hugging, high fiving and if it is the Superbowl, maybe even the random celebration kissing! Some of my favorite flirting happens at home games. Hut, Hut, Hike!

"Friend vs Family"

When your friends have brothers or sisters there are always flirting opportunities around. Some of those siblings may just be pretty cute! Harmless flirting is never a bad thing. You know them well enough that you can get away with saying things you could not to a random girl. I flirt with my brother in law's friends; my friend's brothers flirt with me and vice versa. It is all in good fun. Do not go any further here than the random flirts though unless you want to get married. We don't want to have to choose sides between friends and family and you will always lose out. Blood IS thicker than water after all.

Chapter 9: The Brush Off

Have you ever noticed a woman staring off over your shoulder when you are talking to her? How about you thought you saw her but she made a duck and run to the restroom when you started walking over? Welcome to the brush off. These come from when we just are not that interested and you are not getting the hint, or after we hook up and you all of a sudden are crowding us so close we need to come up for air. Follow these simple rules and you will never be the guy that just will not go away.

1. If I like you, I am making eye contact with you. I am looking you straight in the eye daring you to make a move. Do not think she is just shy and does not want to look you in the eye. What she is doing is scanning the room looking for a way out. Don't force her to make up a bad excuse to get away.
2. If I like you, I am dancing with you. I am smiling at you, moving closer & encouraging you – no matter how badly you dance. If I am moving away from you or trying to put other people between us, I am simply not interested.
3. If I like you, I will compliment you. Do not go fishing comments for me by walking up and asking me if I like your shirt/pants/shoes. If I have noticed you that might be my line to see if you have interest. If you ask me, I may think you are too feminine for a hook-up.
4. If I like you, I might want to talk to you another time. If you ask me for my phone number right off the bat, and I say I do not have paper or a pen, don't go searching one out. If I want to give you that personal information when you ask, I will tell you to hang on a second while I scrounge up a writing utensil. Even if it is lipstick across your arm. If I like you and you ask I will kill myself to make sure you get a way to contact me.

5. If I like you, I am engaging you in conversation. If I am responding in one word answers, I am letting you know I am not interested.
6. If I call you out about other girls you were dancing/talking/flirting with tonight, I am not interested. If I like you, I have noticed you left all them to come talk to me. If I call you out on it, it is because I noticed you were the creepy stalker guy who is working the room waiting for an opening.
7. If we are having casual conversation at the bar & you go off to shoot pool with your buddies, then come back by to tell me which table you're playing just in case I want to say goodbye before I go & I do not stop by nor even look your direction to watch you play; I am not interested. I was being polite.

Chapter 10: Questions NOT To Ask A Hook-Up

The following are actual questions we have been asked. You may even recognize your opening line among the list. These are questions you should not be asking any woman within the first minutes, hours, or days of meeting her. Some may be appropriate once you consider the idea of a relationship… but in context of the tryst, these rules apply.

1. Are you a real blonde? (Brunette? Red head?)
   Guess what? We do know why you ask this question. Guess what? It doesn't work! Don't believe me? Think to yourself for just one moment... When is the last time you used this one & were invited to check for yourself? That's ok, keep thinking. We'll wait.

2. Are they real?
   If you can't already tell, does it really matter? No. Boys like boobs. Boys like ALL boobs. If they aren't real, it's something we have done for ourselves; this has nothing to do with you.

3. Do you have hardwood floors or shag carpet?
   Is this a hook up or a relationship? It's a hook up enjoy the art of discovery! (...and refer back to the answer for question 1, same result.)

4. Do you swallow?
   We're going to tell you a secret. 90% of us do. Most of us actually really, really like it too! Now, whether or not this occurs during a short term fling is still to be determined; so don't ask. If you're lucky you will find out for yourself soon enough. Just know that we expect the same consideration.

5. Was I good?
   If you're asking? The answer is already no.... but you knew that. So stop reading & go practice!

6. Am I big enough?
   Ahh, another of the myths... that women dig on over sized penises. We mentioned it earlier; sex is about quality not quantity. Regardless of length, girth or how long you can hold out, be confident in whom you are sexually & you will be a much bigger turn on!

7. Why aren't you taken?
   Where should I be taken to? Ask a stupid question – get a stupid answer. Believe it or not, not all women are out there to find a relationship. Perhaps one will come along when she least expects it; but we'll knock this one right back at you. Why aren't <u>you</u> taken?

8. How old are you?
   How old do you think I am? If you say 24 I am going to say you are psychic. Why would you ask me to lie to you with your first question?

9. Do you have kids? How old are they?
   Why do you care? Does that make a difference if you get my panties off or not? This is also digging into how old I am, and unless we are dating you will never meet them or know how old I am for that matter...

10. Do you do this often?
    "Why yes, every other day. I am a total slut. How about you?" REALLY??? And just how would you like me to answer this question?

11. How many men have you been with?
    I am not going to tell you how many, how often, or who I have had sex with. I will say you are going to be my first. This is so not ok to ask even if you have been dating for a year unless you want a lie.

12. Do you want children in the future?
    If this is your sneaky way of asking me if it is ok not to wear a condom, the answer is no. It is not OK. Wear your condom every time. The other option here is that you are actually curious about this… for someone who just met me, that's way too forward!

13. How long should someone date before getting married?
    Well that depends. How many carats is the rock you are buying me?

14. Do you believe in love at first sight?
    Absolutely, positively, without a doubt – No! You don't even know the person, how can you love them. And if you are telling me you are in love with me after 10 minutes in a bar, I would seriously consider visiting a therapist. You have a problem.

15. Would you like to have dinner with my parents' tomorrow night?
    Slow down there stallion. I am not the girl you take home to mom. I don't want to be the girl you take home to mom. I want to be the girl you text your friends about at 4am with "OMG, BEST EVER… MY MIND IS BLOWN!"

16. Can we speed this up? My wife will be home in an hour.

Do I even have to respond to this one? Wear a ring for our sanity if you are married guys PLEASE. You owe it to your wife for putting up with a sleaze like you.

17. I would love for my kids to meet you!
Similar to the fact you will never meet mine, I will not be meeting yours. I do not want to play mommy to someone else's bundles of joy. I will not deal with your ex-wife, or change diapers. Can we hurry up to the anonymous sex part?

18. Are you ladies "together"? As in lesbians?
If we were lesbians why would we be here talking to you? If you did not pay attention enough to notice when we are somewhere we scan the room rating the men there, then why should I pay attention enough to consider having sex with you?

19. Would you & your friend do a threesome with me?
Do we have glowing neon signs on our foreheads that say "Come star in your very own porn flick tonight?" (Actually we might, but that does not mean we are doing it together)...

20. Tell me about your family? Job? Hobbies? Friends? ...or anything else that pertains to you caring as more than a passing fling.
Unless you really want to pursue something with a girl, leave this crap out of it. She may be into the hook up – but if you pretend to be interested in these things, she may think you want more than you actually do.

Chapter 11: Pick Up Lines That Don't Work

As ridiculous as they sound, these lines have actually been spoken to us at one point or the other. Do not fall back on some cheesy way to get our attention. Just smile and say hello. It will go so much further to your cause. If you lay one of these doozy's on us, we promise we will TRY not to laugh in your face, no guarantees though.

1. Didn't we meet last night? No? Then you must have been the girl of my dreams!
2. If I told you that you have a beautiful body would you hold it against me?
3. Did it hurt when you fell from heaven?
4. If you were a booger, I'd pick you first!
5. Do you have any Italian in you? Do you want some?
6. If I flip this coin, what are the chances of me getting head?
7. What's your name? Really, that is my Mom's (daughter's, sister's, ex-wife's, dog's etc.) name too!
8. Where is your boyfriend? Wow, you are too beautiful not to have one. Is there something wrong with you I cannot see?
9. Do you come here often?
10. If I were your boyfriend, I would never let you out alone…
11. HEY Beauuuuuutiflulul! (followed by anything slurred)
12. Are you from Germany?
13. How come I have never seen you here before?
14. What time do you have to be home tonight?
15. Does this shirt make me look fat?
16. (As watching a football game in my favorite teams jersey) What team are you rooting for?
17. (If I have my hair in pigtail braids) Is your name Maryanne?
18. Where have you been my whole life?

19. So did you get a ride here or do you have your own car?
20. Can you buy me a drink? I lost my wallet.
21. I am going to the restroom; do you want to escort me?
22. I don't smoke except for when I drink, can I have a cigarette?

One other thing to note… If we have not been speaking, don't walk up to me and try and kiss me, hug me, or put your hands on me in anyway. This is NOT ok!!

Chapter 12 : In Conclusion

This book was written specifically to help all you men out there with your game and to tell you where some (many) men make their fatal flaws that ruin the sport. So go out there and hook up! Just remember with every game there are rules. Some you can wiggle around, some you can bend, some you can break. Most of the time if you break, bend or even wiggle around the rules though, the game changes and then how can you win? If you walk away with anything, just remember these tips:

1. Always make eye contact and smile.
2. Don't be offensive, but be challenging and confident. Show us you are a true man!
3. Dress & groom yourself well to attract our attention.
4. Be witty, and engaging. Make us want to keep talking to you.
5. Above all, when you get us in your bedroom (on the balcony, in the stairwell, in the car, etc.) grab a big handful of our hair at the nape of our necks and pull…

Now get out there and play… **Game On!**

And an important PS... ALWAYS wear a condom.

**** If you have a problem with any sort of STD, go to the Doctor. Go straight to the Doctor. Do not pass go, do not collect $200... It is not nearly as embarrassing as what we will do to you when we find out. Yes things happen but it should be obvious to you if a gal can tell at this point something is going on, you have known for awhile. And when we run into you again don't pretend nothing happened. Women are not dumb. For him to be in his position of authority, we know he was not dumb either. Acknowledge the mistake and move on. We will, just not with you.*

www.ingramcontent.com/pod-product-compliance
Ingram Content Group UK Ltd.
Pitfield, Milton Keynes, MK11 3LW, UK
UKHW041914190726
13854UKWH00003B/1250

9 781105 513022